Dancing with Chaos

Patricia Monaghan

*To Flo and
Scott —
fellow dancers!
love Patricia
2002*

salmonpoetry

Published in 2002 by
Salmon Publishing Ltd,
Cliffs of Moher, Co. Clare, Ireland
www.salmonpoetry.com
email: info@salmonpoetry.com

A catalogue record for this book is available from the British Library.

ISBN 1 903392 27 6

Cover artwork: 'Justice' by Eleanor Lundquist
Cover design & typesetting by Siobhán Hutson

ACKNOWLEDGEMENTS

Grateful acknowledgement is made to the following journals in which some of these poems, or earlier versions of them, first appeared:

Janus Head, River Oak Review, and *Power Lines: Ten Years of Poetry from Chicago's Guild Complex*

The inspiration for this book came from the encouragement of my doctoral committee: Joe Meeker, Ryn Etter, Miriam Dexter, Michael Miner and Natalie Kusz. Students at DePaul University have challenged me to articulate the concepts of chaos, and Etta Worthington and River Oak Arts welcomed this work in its early stages.

CONTENTS

In the Beginning   *11*

I

Laminar Flow   15
White Silences   16
Dark Matter   17
The Butterfly Tattoo Effect   18
Examination   20
Answer Sheet   21
Broken Symmetry   23
Nothing is Ever Simultaneous   24
Degrees of Freedom   26
Strange Attractor   28

II

By Accident   33
The Three-Body Problem   34
The Fractal Geometry of Love   36
Gifts, Not Promises   38
Desideratum   39
Your Hair   40
Your Skin   41
Your Hands, Your Feet   43
Your Mouth   44
Your Voice   45
Your Eyes, At that Moment   47
Bell's Theorem: Epithalamion   49

III

Mandelbrot Set   53
Guardians at the Gates   56

Seven Elementary Catastrophes   57
Fibonacci Stevens   58
Observations of Schrödinger's Cat   60
An Associated Medium   63
Hurricanes in Spacetime   65
Higgs' Bos'n   67
Falling Bodies   70
Shiva to Kali, on the Charnel Ground   71
Kali to Shiva, on the Charnel Ground   72
Ecstasy   73
The Poised Edge of Chaos   77

Glossary   *81*

In the Beginning
— *After Ovid*

Before land, sea, sky, before all that:
nature was chaos; our cosmos, all chaos;
all the same enormity, all in one;
there was no form, no moon to walk
the night, no earth to dance with air,
no ocean touching shimmeringly
the fractal reefs and particulate sand;
life and lifelessness the same,
roughness, smoothness the same,
heat falling into cold, cold into heat,
dampness falling into drought,
heaviness falling into weightlessness,
yieldingness falling into adamant.

Now let me tell you how things change,
new rising endlessly out of old,
everything altering, form unto form,
let me be the voice of mutability,
the only constant in this world.

I

LAMINAR FLOW

A: A violent order is disorder, and
B: A great disorder is an order.
These two things are one.
     — Wallace Stevens

We were driving. You were silent.
I had given up speaking and sat watching
out the window as the hedgerows flew by.
You wanted to drive to the top of a hill
to see a chapel. Or perhaps it was I who
wanted that. We were driving, in any case.
In my memory, we are often that way:
driving.   Not speaking, just driving.

That time I was remembering a farmer
who had loved me. Loved me and sent me
away, back to you. I missed his nakedness.
You were never naked with me. Your eyes
were always cloaked, your heart shrouded.

There was some confusion, I remember.
Something about a wrong turn along the way,
at the bottom of the hill. Finally we found
the chapel, a charming place beside a pleasant
overlook above a river. Children ran laughing
along the paths. There was nothing wrong.
There was absolutely nothing wrong.

DARK MATTER

A cave with no walls.
The eye of destruction.

A raven at midnight in winter.
The reservoir of namelessness.

Everything I had forgotten I remember.
The parts of my heart that broke away.

WHITE SILENCES

Beyond geography. Beyond blood.
Beyond latitude. Beyond salt.

Beyond continents. Beyond tears.
That kind of coldness.

My hair is beaded with crystals.
Forgetful and aloof, I am slipping

into white silences, becoming
cold skin over hard finality.

THE BUTTERFLY TATTOO EFFECT

Does the flap of a butterfly's wings in Brazil set off a tornado in Texas?
— Edward Lorenz

Charlene was fifty when she got it:
one small butterfly, perched on
her right shoulder, bright blue
with stipples of pink. Everything
in her life seemed safe by then:
husband, children, house and dog.
She wanted to be a little dangerous.

When she left the Jade Dragon
she called her oldest friend, Maggie,
in Florida, with the news. A tattooed
gal at fifty, she bragged. I ain't down yet.

Maggie laughed that throaty laugh of hers.
An hour later on her way to work,
she stopped on a whim and bought
a gallon of red paint for her door.
That night, she didn't drive straight
home but stopped for a drink at an old
haunt from her more dangerous years.
No one she knew was there, so she talked
awhile to Flo, the bartender, told her about
feng shui and red doors, and oh yes, she
mentioned the tattoo just before she left.

It rested in Flo's mind all night as she
uncapped the beers and mixed the drinks.
She was warmer than usual, sassy and loud.
Things got wild. There was dancing.
A new woman stopped in and picked up
one of the regulars. Washing up past midnight,

Flo thought of her old friend Paula, who
lived in California. It was still early there.

Flo picked up the phone, right then,
and called. Somehow the subject of Charlene's
tattoo came up. Paula had been thinking
of getting one too. Why not? Life marks us all,
why can't we chose our scars just once?
They talked till late. The next day Paula
walked into a dealership and bought
the reddest car she saw. By nightfall she was
driving fast, towards the south. And the next morning

the world awoke to news of seismic convulsions
on every continent brought on by
the simultaneous shifting into high gear
of millions of women in sleek red cars.

EXAMINATION

1. Describe disruption of laminar flow.
2. Is uncertainty random?
3. Are unpredictable instabilities chaotic?
4. Distinguish between noise and chaos.
5. Is chance further reducible?
6. Are all attractors strange?
7. Draw a basin of attraction.
8. Name a useful dissipative system.
9. Can a stable equilibrium last?
10. How turbulent is the heart?

ANSWER SHEET

1. In the wilderness
   between centre and edge
   the vortex is born.
2. Distinguish between
   not knowing
   and not knowing:
   one at the root of all,
   one an order
   so immense we
   have to stand
   in another universe
   to glimpse its outline.
3. Wait. Long. Enough.
4. A: Distantly I hear
   water dropping
   onto porcelain.
   B: Inside
   explosions
   are instants
   of silence.
5. The weakness
   of the theory:
   the constancy
   of "chance,"
   Einstein said,
   which "does not
   get us any closer."
6. A boulder.
   Two gold pins.
   Three feathers.
   And then:
   an owl,
   flying,

flying away,
flying far away.

7. My hands tracing
the hollow of your throat.

8. Abandoned to the dance.

9. Instead, recurrence:
never the same thing exactly,
never exactly the same,
but repeating the same thing,
never exactly the same thing,
but repeating, recurring, repeating.

10. As any instrument
that translates
noise, chaos
into
music, order.

BROKEN SYMMETRY

We could never dance
because he would neither
lead nor follow.

Awkward, angry, he
would push me around
the dance floor.

Eager and angry, I would
change my steps trying
to match his.

When all hope was lost,
he advanced on me, and
I of course retreated.

NOTHING IS EVER SIMULTANEOUS

Two friends take a walk in a park.
Stopping at its centre, they synchronize
watches and agree upon a time to meet.

One walks swiftly. The other dawdles.
One covers miles, the other sits beside
a splashing fountain. Hours later,
they reunite, and one is late: the one
who raced through the park, the one
in motion. The other's watch — the one
who dawdled — shows a different time,
faster by the breadth of a mouse's whisker.

The next time these friends go to the park,
they carry ornate golden watches, precisely
accurate. The same thing happens.
One is late, a little late. The same one,
the faster one. The friends then
borrow atomic watches, those perfect
timekeepers. The same thing happens.
The same thing always happens.

> I am moving, flying through
> caverns of sharp spruce where
> dark birds have nested
> for a hundred centuries,
>
> I am swimming towards
> a dark blue cavern where
> there are carvings that show
> the exact trajectory of light
> that strikes an eye just before
> it closes forever,

I am running, my legs flowing
under me like water, my eyes
burning in stinging wind,
and somewhere in front of me
there is a granite mountain
that beats like a heart —

We go walking in a park.
Two paths lead from the perimeter
through the wild forest.
We have identical compasses.
We have identical maps.
We have perfect watches.
We agree to meet at the fountain.
We specify a meeting time.
We each choose a path.

I am, at this moment, walking in a direction
you cannot imagine, you who judge everything
in terms of forward motion, you who imagine me
unmoving, waiting as you pass through my world
like a brilliant burning comet, leaving faint periodic
traces in a spiral galaxy: I am opening inward,

spiralling towards nothingness and truth,
moving in no direction you can imagine,
opening like an expanding universe
with no unmoving point within it.

We never see each other again.

DEGREES OF FREEDOM

a
pen–
dulum
can only
swing (no
matter how
fast how slow) can
only swing in that
small space (no matter
how fast how slow,
no matter) it can
only swing

one

degree

one
degree
of freedom,

that is what it is
called, that limit cycle,
(back & forth, no matter,
back & forth, fast and slow):
one degree of freedom

But

there is a way
to get more

there is a way
to move

there is a way
to reach
infinite

degrees of
freedom:

move   towards
        chaos,   move
                towards   change,
                move   towards

turbulence

                        there
        are   so
                        many
                                degrees
                                of
                                freedom
                                                        there
                        so
                                                                many
                                degrees
                        uncounted
                                uncountable
        a   rolling   ring
                                of
                                freedom

        so   many

        degrees
                                        of
                                        freedom
        this   close

                                to
                                        chaos

STRANGE ATTRACTOR

A long rain falling on a late spring day, a fact
That seems significant in retrospect — open
Road ahead, looming sky, slashing wind —
Me driving vaguely east, towards someplace
Clear enough on the map. All the verges
Green and slick, dangerous, flash flood

Warning on the radio. All in flux
When just hours before everything was flat,
Predictable. Weather grained my vision.
I think I was anticipating what would happen.
Earlier that day I blurted out the simplest
Of truths at that kind of knotty moment when

Silence is the only safety. I didn't want
To be safe, that moment, though it was a fluke
I felt that way, I tended to invest my surplus
Fears in stocks of constraint. The sky grew black
As I drove along pondering what gate I'd opened
To the future, telling myself it was a valid

Question, flooded with premonitions of vanished
Comfort, order, reserve. If I had known what
Was happening, what was about to happen,
Would I have turned around and tried my luck
Back home? I doubt it. That moment, tiny fractal
Of my soul, I needed a different kind of solace.

In retrospect, everything so clear, simplicity
Itself, the pattern of my life leading inevitably
To the rending of the fabric, the accident
That changed everything, the sudden bend
In a previously-straight road, the lack,
Suddenly, of directional signs, no option

But to continue in the rain, in the opaque
Light, no option but to travel through sorrow
Until some destination that might prove lucky
If not happy, no option but to go vagrant
From my old safe life, no option but to wend
My way towards some invisible and strange attractor:

As the sky went dark and opal, I vanished
Into someplace torn and darned with wind,
Buoyed upon the flood right up to the impact —

II

BY ACCIDENT

— *From the Chinese Book of Songs*

The hills are covered with soft grass.
Dew is a sweet blanket there each dawn.
Once there was a lovely man
with eyes like water, clear and sweet.
We met by accident. He loved me well.

The hills are covered with the softest grass.
How sweetly the dew lies there each dawn!
Once there was a lovely man
with eyes like clear sweet water.
We met by accident. Oh, he gave me joy.

THE THREE-BODY PROBLEM

These things are so strange
I cannot bear to contemplate them.
　　　　　— Henri Poincaré

It was easy to figure out when there
were just two: me, you. Easy, remember?
The route between us, always starting
here, ending there. Me to you. Never
the other way: starting there, ending here.
Pattern set, route established. We knew
what to expect, how to act. We thought
we knew everything about the future.

Ah, the future. It would be the same; route
set, pattern established. We knew how
everything moved, me to you, one of us
a satellite and one a sun, one peripheral
to the other's centre, me drawing the same
circles around you, over and over. Easy.

But then suddenly, as we were looping
our usual loop, me to you, me to you —
suddenly, there was the other. A new body.
A third. Me, you, the other. What would we
do now? Where were the centres, how could
the circles be drawn, who was to move how?

Two bodies, then a third.

This could have been many stories,
even one as simple as two friends,
having coffee one morning, who
make space for someone to join them,

after which their conversation falters.
Each of us has many such stories.

Two bodies, then a third.
And everything is different after that.

This is one of those stories. This is
the story in which the third body
is one with arms that reach and hold,
eyes that gleam and smile, a body with
all the parts a body needs to come
between other bodies. That story.

No one can predict what will happen
when a third body joins a two-body
system. Linear equations are useless.
One thing is certain: things will change.
We could not go on as before, just another
loop added, once an opening had been made

for chaos —

When three bodies interact, everything
becomes important. Huge changes are caused
by the tiniest gestures: a glance, a whisper,
the touch of fingertips on the inside of a wrist.

Two bodies, then a third.
And everything is different after that.

THE FRACTAL GEOMETRY OF LOVE

> *Clouds are not spheres, mountains are not cones, coastlines*
> *are not circles and bark is not smooth, nor does lightning*
> *travel in a straight line.*
> — Benoit Mandelbrot

1. *Iteration*

There is a kind of hunger
that satisfaction intensifies:

I touch you, I touch you again,
and again, and again, and again,

and with each touch I want
to touch you more, I am caught

in this feedback loop of touching and
touching and touching and touching —

2. *Self-Similarity*

The smallest gesture
is the same as the largest:

when you placed your hand
on mine in that café, it was

the same as when you place
your hand on mine in bed

and when you look into my eyes
for a flashing instant, it is the same

as when you hold them until
we both burst into flame.

3. *Measurement*

The eye is not a sphere.
My breasts are not cones.
Your nipples are not circles.
Your face is not smooth, and
nothing between us
travels in a straight line.

If I were to attempt to
outline your sweet body,
I would be unable to do so:

if I touch it closely enough, so
closely that I trace each cell,
each cell's boundary, each
cell's connection to other
cells, I would be measuring

your outline until the end
of time. And that is what
I am doing, lying here
next to you in the sun,

trying to move beyond time,
beginning my journey
to the infinite, my hand
slowly, slowly, slowly, tracing
the vast outline of your body.

GIFTS, NOT PROMISES

a red silk cord for your neck
horizontal rain with no wind

giving like taking
yielding like gathering

a small soft stone
a petrified blue egg

memories like dreams
dreams like memories

a vial of indigo
a cricket on the bed

DESIDERATUM

Sharp cheese and sour apples.
Your teeth, barely open.

Juice of French nectarines.
Your lips on my arm.

Balsam on the spring wind.
Thick scent of your hair.

Sea otter fur and silk.
Your copper skin.

A red sun in winter.
The hollow of your spine.

The dark note of drums.
Your fire kiss.

A hidden waterfall.
Your pulsing seed.

Alpenglow and a full moon.
Your eyes, at that moment.

Mushrooms after rain.
The salt of us.

A distant windchime.
Your voice, murmuring.

YOUR HAIR

Here is what I would do
if you were next to me:

First I would touch your hair.
I would weave my hands

into your hair. I would stroke
your hair. I would tug slightly

at your hair. I would measure
the length of your hair against

my face and my arm. I would
divide it into strands and braid it.

I would place my mouth against
the ends of the braid and suck.

Unbraiding, I would arrange
a sunburst around your brown face.

I would array your hair like petals
curling out from your brown face.

I would twist it into ringlets
to hang beside your sweet face.

I would cover your face with it.
Then I would uncover your face

and cover it again with my own
hair, and cover it again and again,

sweeping my hair over yours
until the boundaries between

us dissolve as our hair tangles
together, sleek with love and sweat.

YOUR SKIN

if my eyes
were arrows
your skin
would be
torn and rent

    slashed open
    lacerated

if my hands
bled ink
your skin
would be
drawn

    completely
    with spirals

if my fingers
were needles
your skin
would be
embroidered

    with crewel
    dark stitches

if my lips
were thorns
your skin
would be
bleeding

bleeding
bleeding

if my tongue
were a knife
your skin
would be
scarred

pierced
tattooed

YOUR HANDS, YOUR FEET

The extremities are not far,
after all, from the heart:

with your eloquent hands
you tell me what you desire,

what you demand, you talk
to every part of me, your hands

make endless conversation
with my hands, my skin, my lips;

and your feet are just as eloquent,
for when you touch a single toe

against my ankle I can feel your
exploring mind, your wild curiosity,

your desperate need for warmth,
your innocence and fear and lust,

and when your foot pushes between
my feet, and stretches itself out

so that your leg can press mine open
I need no other eloquence except,

perhaps, your hands, your hands,
pressing me in an extremity of joy.

YOUR MOUTH

It is high summer.
I am a salmon.

Yours is the only
mouth I know,

the only mouth
I recognize as home.

*

There is a music
wilder than the pipes.

It is what your mouth
plays on my breast.

*

Sometimes when you
speak I do not listen:

I watch the way
you taste your words.

I watch the way
you drink the air.

*

Your mouth sings
without language

when it finds mine.
My song answers.

YOUR VOICE

Now let me praise your voice
which is, of all your beauties, most
like magic. To hear it in your absence,

I must conjure golden darknesses:
smoke of sassafras, old amber,
burnt cream and honeyed brandy,

the border between sunset and night.
If my soul had skin, your voice would be
a knife of bronze, cutting me to shreds,

for you name in the rich darkness
all the women I have ever been,
little girl, mama, baby, oh my girl,

like conjured ghosts they flicker
and are gone, return, are gone,
return again, are gone —

and then you rock me, crooning,
having known all of me, having
loved all of me, letting me gather

all the shards of self and wash them
in the pool of memory, your voice
a liquor that dissolves false bonds

and then restores. And later, in
the most ordinary circumstance,
your voice cuts into me like the wild

thin sound of pipes, for the ghosts
gather even in the daylight, awaiting
even the slightest word, conjured

by just an inflection, just a syllable.
Your voice glows with the power
of old rites and older rituals,

of invocation and of exorcism.
Voice of dark gold, of sassafras
and amber, let me sing your praise.

YOUR EYES, AT THAT MOMENT

Now let me praise your eyes.

Not for their beauty, which is like
amber or jasper or flecked agate.
Not for their steadiness, which is like
village drums on a hot night.
Not for their clarity, which is like
sunlight on the arctic ocean.

Not for the way they see through
lies. Not for the way they penetrate
masks. Not for the way they pierce
the armour around the heart.

Nor will I praise the way your eyes
can see the invisible: bird spirits
in the crowns of trees, the shape
of wind on a stormy sea, an owl's
night flight, a spent rainbow.

I will not praise your eyes
for any of this or all, I will not
praise your eyes for anything

except that one moment when
at your peak of pleasure
your eyes grow more naked
than even your brown body,
when you pour into me not
just your body's essence but
your soul's, when you let me

see, for just one moment, all

the truth of sex: salmon roiling
in the seas, a cat screaming
in the night, ravens flying wing
to wing, the tearing pain of birth,
death's immeasurable release.

All this, in your eyes.
Your eyes, at that moment.
Praise be. Praise be.

BELL'S THEOREM: AN EPITHALAMION

Forget for a moment
this man and this woman.
Forget the sun and water.
Forget the brightening sky.
Forget the dimming stars.
Forget the half moon
yearning towards its fullness.
Forget everything

except the soil.

I could say many things of it:
I could say that soil is like
the time a man and woman
spend together, the moments
fragmentary and invisible that
sustain them. I could say
that soil is time, moments
upon moments upon moments,
each necessary, none identical —

but let the soil be soil,
not a metaphor
for love or time,
let it be what it is:
millions of particles
scoured from pebbles
torn from mountains
by passing glaciers,

and bits of mammoth bone,
shards from an old woman's pot,
fragments of leaf from a tree

beneath which lovers sang,
all within the soil,

and even more:

half of an electron, split
apart in the centre of the sun,
its other self somewhere across
the galaxy, boiling in vapour or
frozen in rock,

and if you could
blow upon the fragment here,
could turn it in its tiny dance,
its distant other would turn
at that same instant, still embraced
in an old inferno of connection —

After this day, when this man flies,
this woman flies. When she dances,
he dances. What touches one
affects the other. No galaxy can separate
what has been joined here on this day.

III

MANDELBROT SET

..disorder, on which order floats...
— Ilya Prigogine

1. The Heart

The dark interior of the heart
shatters in a certain way:

it breaks in two,
and breaks again in two,
and breaks again in two,
and again, and again, and
ultimately disintegrates into
dust, infinitely many particles

in which each one is
a tiny replica of the whole.

2. Connected Circles

They look stable and firm.
They look like they will
withstand all dissolution.

They look well-matched.
They look as though they are
so content, so much at peace.

Whatever seems contained
like that is something that
refuses to escape to infinity —

3. Invisible Miniatures

In an ocean of chaos
seeds float like plankton:

what whale feeds here?
what porpoise?

4. The Border

Here is where chaos starts.

It is the fiercest hunger.
It is a great tearing pain
that so occupies the mind
that there is nothing else.

It is being breathed.
It is being breathless.

Standing on the border
of chaos means standing
in a sharp cold wind
on the highest pass
in arctic mountains.

It means plunging
into stars.
It means soaring
into jade seas.

Here at the border
we are not in chaos yet.
This is more relentless
than chaos. And

more beautiful. Far,
far more beautiful.

5. *The Chaotic Regime*

If order hides
   in the folds
of apparent disorder,

   where is chaos hiding?

At the furthest distance
   from order
where everything becomes

   infinite
all at once,
instantly,

   I am looking for chaos

and
floating above it at

   the greatest height

I can see

      a raven

spread its wings
and

   fly

GUARDIANS AT THE GATES

Dragons are dancing
at the edges of chaos.

Their eyes are mouths.
They eat us whole.

I am being devoured
by dragon eyes.

I am falling forever
into a jewelled maze.

I am being pierced
all over with light.

Pain flays me awake.
I taste my blood.

I slept once, wrapped
in soft white comfort.

I cannot imagine
ever sleeping again.

SEVEN ELEMENTARY CATASTROPHES

Poetry is a perfectly possible means of overcoming chaos.
  –I.A. Richards

1

Born female,
in wartime,
under the full moon
of mid-winter.

2

I see a wild onion in a field.
It is the first I have ever seen.
I recognize it instantly.

3

The first time I mistake
a mountain for a cloud.

4

In my dream, a nameless
horse. I try to capture it.
Over and over and over.

5

A black dog steps
from the forest.
I do not run away.

6

I go to the holy mountain.
Its head is soft with clouds.
I set my foot upon the path.

7

I am offered a tiny gift.
I do not refuse.

FIBONACCI STEVENS

Chaos
is
the law
of ideas, of
improvisations and seasons of belief.

And
yet
relation appears,
a small relation:

This
object
is merely
a state, one
of many, between two poles,
so, in the metaphysical, there are these poles:

Nothing
exists
by itself.

Ramon
Fernandez
tell me
if you know
why, when the singing ended
and we turned towards the town, tell why
the glassy lights, the lights in the fishing boats at anchor

were
falling
like notes
from a piano.

Thus
the
constant violets,
doves, girls, bees
and hyacinths are inconstant objects
of inconstant cause in a universe of inconstancy.

OBSERVATIONS OF SCHRÖDINGER'S CAT

When it comes to atoms, language can only be used as poetry. The poet,
too, is not nearly so concerned with describing facts as with creating images.
— Neils Bohr

When I'm in the box,
what I hear mostly is
the sound of my own body:
little rifflings, twisted
roars, sometimes a whirr.
And smell, I notice that —
my own warm smell
I mean — the box is thick, too
thick for anything outside
to make its way to me.

I can feel, too, the edges
of my body, my claws
with their uneven points,
my hard paws, my little
antennae whiskers. I know
I am spotted, black and white,
because I can feel the tiny
difference between my colours:
black like putty or molasses,
white slick as oily paint
against my sandy tongue.

There's nothing to do here
but play with the device —
that little poison toy that
you imagine I ignore —
and so I do. I roll it over
and over, press my nose
against it, even toss it

in the air now and again.
My fate is randomly controlled.
And so I play. I might as well.

Of course I grow hungry
and thirsty, but these
experiments are brief,
I'm out in time for meals.
And then I'm at the dish
instantly, and you think
I'm not listening as
you talk about my life,
the way you have created
me, the way I'm only here
because you witness me,

and when I arch my back
and purr, and you stroke me
and think I'm ignorant while
you are not — I'm laughing
at your theories. Really,
you have missed it all.

Put this into your formulae:
I see myself in risky
darknesses, I am my own
witness to my life, I do
not live or die because
you watch. Put this in too:

sometimes my solitude expands
the space between the nucleus
and electrons of every atom
until I am vast, floating cloudlike
over you, watching you go about
your other experiments, floating

over the ocean like a hurricane,
floating out into space, observing
everything at the same instant.

And if one day you find me
dead in my little box, you will
never know what that means,
whether I am gone like a snuffed
light, or whether I am still roving
among the dim and distant stars.

AN ASSOCIATED MEDIUM

Wave fields always propagated in a medium…each field
necessarily had an associated medium.
— Heinz Pagels

She was dressed in violet velvet, long and loose.
On her shoulders, like epaulets, were ripples
of something like water, but not flowing, just rippling.
Embroidered insignia paraded across her sash,
denoting all her orders and associations and honours.
There was something turbanlike on her head, though
in the soft darkness it might have been the shadow of a halo.
She was surrounded by mirrors, so there seemed to be
many of her, even when I looked straight into her eyes.

I am not foolish enough to believe in futures, at least
not in ones that could be foretold, so I do not know why
I sought her out in her tent in the centre of the field.
I don't know why I'm telling you this, even now, in fact.
Something that she said haunts me so. I tell this story
to strangers like you, even when I don't want to.

But it's not a story, though, not really. Call it an incident.
An anecdote. A moment in the sweep of planetary space
that was different, just a little, from moments that
preceded and followed it. Or, perhaps, not different at all.

At the outset, let me say, I thought I knew my way around.
Hell, more than thought. I was confident. Cocksure.
I could loose an arrow and watch it travel through the air
right to my target. I could build a fire and boil water
and never wonder how the heat got through the pot.
Something touched something, something moved
through something, it was all so obvious and simple.

But sitting there, watching her flicker like a candle,
seeming to be on one side, or in the mirror, or over
at the other side, I lost my bearings. She nodded once,
as though she knew just what I wanted, and then leaned
over something — I'd like to say a crystal ball, but I
couldn't see anything on the dark velvet of the table —
and then there was a long pause, and then she spoke.

That was all. I went to the dark field, I went to her tent,
I sat down, she looked at something, and then she spoke.

Not much of a story, is it? I don't know why I need
to tell it like this, even to strangers like you. Something
about that night. Something about her face, flickering.
Something about the way everything afterwards —

What's that? Oh, what she said? Oh yes. Oh, yes.

HURRICANES IN SPACETIME

The winds splintered the house
in which I kept the calendar
passed down to me from Mayan
architects and bardic Irish sailors
and crushed it into rubble.
That calendar had been the only way
I knew when the sun would rise
and when the moon would set.
Beneath the canopy of laden clouds,
night and day were the same.
Without the calender, time
was both a moment and forever.

Without that guide, I had no
reason to stay, and so I departed.
I walked as far as I could. When
I grew tired, I slept, then walked
again under the clouds. I walked
around the world, I think, if you
believe the world is round. Here,
not far I think from where I started,
I joined these priests who raise
foundlings until they are old enough
to become priests or be abandoned.

I do not know why I did not become
a priest like those who found me.
I wore their robes, tying them each
morning with the vines I'd harvested
since childhood. I ate their heavy
gruel and thin vegetable stock, the dark
bread and the thin wafers. I grew up
without love but without pain either.

But when the time came to choose, I shook
my head at the chance to stay. And so I
was abandoned on this island where no one
has ever been seen once the coracle drifts away.

And you?   What brought you to this place?

HIGGS' BOS'N

I was looking for space
big enough to store three chests
of balls made right here in Cork
by Mr. Mark, when I saw him.
I'd run into him in Galway
earlier this year, in a dark
pub on the Claddagh field.
I could barely see his face
that time: the no-you-must
smoke and the sure-I-will
drink, you know, I could
barely see anything but
distant lights of coracles out
the little window of the snug.

But I'd'a known him anywhere,
that lug of a body on him,
I've never seen a man so big.
I could have played poker
on his chest, I swear. With three
friends. Four. That would be it:
four. Sitting around him, him
splayed out flat on the deck,
us around him like a picnic table.

He was that big.

So there he was, leaning
like a tree, no, like a tilting
ship, no, like a whole horizon —
there he was leaning against
the very cabin I was renting
to store my goods. All those

balls of cork. Did I say cork?
I meant from Cork. Yes, yes.

Oh, so what did he say,
that continent of a fella, that
entire sky of a man, what
do you think he suggested?

"I made this shed myself,"
he said — my shed! My little
cork ball storage shed!
"Mr. Higgs wanted it.
That's my job. Higgs wants it,
I make it. That's my job."

Well I can tell you I didn't
take the time of day from
that one, I passed him by
like he was invisible as air —
well, air can have smoke in it
and you can see the curving
patterns then, but I mean
clean sea air, not pub air,
but you know that — so he

puts out his big arm, his arm
like a boulder, and he touches
me, and what do you think
he says then, the bold one:

he says, "All it takes is Higgs
to say it, and it's as good as done.
I have to move around a lot,
you know, but he's the captain.
I don't remember" — he said this,
said this to *me* would you believe —

"I don't remember him ordering
you. When did I make you?
When did I make those balls?"

He's blithering, man, doxy.
Crazy. Big and crazy. Like he
could make a man like an old
shed piled up from rotten timbers.
Like he could carve the little
balls of cork in their nice nests,
three at a whirl. Crazy.

But Chrissakes, is he big.

FALLING BODIES

Feathers and cannon,
planets and string,
all fall together
at the same speed:

falling bodies seem
simple unless you are one
of the dancers falling
toward each other:

Who will be feather?
Who will be planet?
Will we land together
on the sturdy earth?

Each time we move
we fall into time.
Dancing is simply
falling with grace.

SHIVA TO KALI, ON THE CHARNEL GROUND

Your lily feet! Your sweet red feet!
I feel them pounding on me,

pounding my chestbone, breaking
my heart in its case of bone,

breaking my bones, breaking my spine,
crushing me into rags and blood. Ecstasy.

Ecstasy. This is more than joy, this
moment of annihilation as you rip

out my heart and drink my blood,
as you cut off your head and throw it

to the wailing dogs. As your sweet feet
make music on my dying body, I open

everything I ever closed to you so
that you may leave nothing untouched

or undestroyed, I am not offering myself
for any other reason than to offer myself,

and because only as I am destroyed
will I finally know who I have been.

KALI TO SHIVA, ON THE CHARNEL GROUND

The eye is a curious organ.

It blinks, and everything stops.

It blinks, and the world disappears.

You blinked.

I never stopped dancing.

ECSTASY

You have come to this tavern of ruin
where the drunk wine is sweet
and the sung song is ecstasy.
What will become of you now?
— Barbara Flaherty

1

It came upon me the first time in the forest.
I looked up into the sunshine and,
in that moment, I was dismembered.

It was as though a hammer of cold lead
had broken some crystal skin I did not know
I wore. I shattered into pieces. But I was still
whole. I shattered again. And again. Over
and over. I shattered and shattered.

Each time, I thought the space between myself
and the world had disappeared. Each time,
I discovered it had not. Each time,

I came closer to disappearing.

2

After that, I sought it.

I sought it everywhere and at all times and in all ways.

3

But I did not find it.

Not finding it, I went to sleep.

4

Years passed and I forgot.

I forgot about the way obsidian
both breaks and is shattered.
I forgot my obsidian soul.

I did not even know that
I had forgotten. Years passed.
I did not miss my soul.

And then, on a gray lake
on a pale summer day,
it flew back into me like
a raven across the water.

I was the raven, I was the water,
I was the sky, I was the night
that hid within the day, I was
the day just past and the one to come,
I was all things and all times at once.

I never forgot again.

5
It would not come when bidden
but I, being willful, wished it to:

There were moments in the smoked light
of dark bars, when the music was too loud,
when for an instant the drums would steal
my soul away and replace it with themselves.

There were moments in the pale dawn
when to my exhausted eye the world revealed
a great serenity and order, then shifted
just as suddenly into randomness and pain.

Willful, demanding, I risked everything
and lost much, and only sometimes won.

6

And then came grace.

Grace with a body.

Grace with tender eyes.

Grace with fierceness.

Grace with endurance.

Grace like a horse in a dream.

Grace like blood in the mouth.

7

After that, I sought grace everywhere.
Everywhere, at all times, in all men.
Everywhere, willful, demanding, everywhere.

8

What cannot be controlled will not be.
What cannot be earned will not be.

I stopped believing and invested
everything I had in the Bank of Order.

Dividends were certain, I thought.
There would be no more risk.

There would be no more pain.
There would be no more grace.

And there was not. There was not.
There was only the plain, level

and endless, on which I lived.
There were no mountains anywhere.

9

When grace comes
it can come dancing

or slashing and slamming
and tearing and cutting

finally it came
not dancing

10

the drums
the fire
the mountains

the whale
the sun
the flower

the moment
of complete
nakedness

the moment
of complete
emptiness

the fire
the drums
the mountains

11

Now
I seek it nowhere.

Now
I find it everywhere.

THE POISED EDGE OF CHAOS

Sand sifts down, one grain at a time,
forming a small hill.   When it grows high
enough, a tiny avalanche begins.   Let
sand continue to sift down, and avalanches
will occur irregularly, in no predictable order,
until there is a tiny mountain range of sand.
Peaks will appear, and valleys, and as
sand continues to descend, the relentless
sand, piling up and slipping down, piling
up and slipping down, piling up — eventually
a single grain will cause a catastrophe, all
the hills and valleys erased, the whole face
of the landscape changed in an instant.

Walking yesterday, my heels crushed chamomile
and released intoxicating memories of home.
Earlier this week, I wrote an old love, flooded
with need and desire.   Last month I planted
new flowers in an old garden bed —

one grain at a time, a pattern is formed,
one grain at a time, a pattern is destroyed,
and there is no way to know which grain
will build the tiny mountain higher, which
grain will tilt the mountain into avalanche,
whether the avalanche will be small or
catastrophic, enormous or inconsequential.

We are always dancing with chaos, even when
we think we move too gracefully to disrupt
anything in the careful order of our lives,
even when we deny the choreography of passion,
hoping to avoid earthquakes and avalanches,

turbulence and elemental violence and pain.
We are always dancing with chaos, for the grains
sift down upon the landscape of our lives, one,
then another, one, then another, one then another.

Today I rose early and walked by the sea,
watching the changing patterns of the light
and the otters rising and the gulls descending,

and the boats steaming off into the dawn,
and the smoke drifting up into the sky,
and the waves drumming on the dock,

and I sang. An old song came upon me,
one with no harbour nor dawn nor dock,
no woman walking in the mist, no gulls,
no boats departing for the salmon shoals.

I sang, but not to make order of the sea
nor of the dawn, nor of my life. Not to make
order at all. Only to sing, clear notes over sand.
Only to walk, footsteps in sand. Only to live.

Glossary

LAMINAR FLOW: The slickness that precedes turbulence.

DARK MATTER: There is not enough mass in the universe. Some of it — indeed much of it — appears to be missing. This missing matter is believed to be so dense that it does not reflect light.

BUTTERFLY EFFECT: Newton's laws suggest that a small cause has a small effect and that, conversely, a large effect demands a large cause. Chaos theory proves otherwise.   When a motion is iterated through a system, a feedback loop can be set in motion. Thus an enormous result can be attained through relatively small originating action.

BROKEN SYMMETRY: Mathematically, symmetry defines situations where something remains unchanged even if we transform it by moving it about; a sphere, for instance, can be moved in any direction and does not change. Such is not the case when symmetry is broken.

DEGREES OF FREEDOM: This is the mathematical term for the number of degrees which a body can move around its fixed point. Near chaos, there are infinite degrees of freedom.

STRANGE ATTRACTOR: In the mathematics of chaos, some nonlinear equations never settle down around fixed attracting points but move, not randomly but in a wild, unpredictable, strange pattern, as though following a moving point.   When charted, the strange attractor's shape looks like an owl's face.

THREE-BODY PROBLEM: At the end of the 19th century, the mathematician Henri Poincaré calculated the answer to a famous problem: how can we calculate the motions of three bodies in movement around each other? Poincaré determined that linear equations — ones in which actions have linear reactions — cannot solve such problems. Rather, nonlinear equations, in which actions can generate geometric reactions, are necessary.

FRACTAL GEOMETRY: Benoit Mandelbrot was a pioneer in defining a new geometry, the first since Euclid. He argues that the world is not filled with circles and triangles and measurable lines, but with broken forms that repeat themselves at different scales.

BELL'S THEOREM: The Irish physicist John Stewart Bell showed that a subatomic particle, split in two, shows parallel reactions to changes in spin no matter how distant its pieces are. This puzzle has not been theoretically solved, because it seems to imply superluminary speed of data communicated between the particles. Although experimentally supported by A. Aspect at CERN's particle accelerator, Bell's Theorem remains controversial.

MANDELBROT SET: Mandelbrot has drawn a design that permits us to visualize chaos. A dark shape — a heart, connected to two balls — is surrounded by marvellously complex shapes, which in turn are surrounded by filaments leading out to colourful zones of abstraction. The Mandelbrot Set shows graphically that the greatest complexity lies at the edges of chaos.

ELEMENTARY CATASTROPHES: These are mathematical equivalents of choice, points at which the answer determines the next set of functions.

SCHRÖDINGER'S CAT: Erwin Schrödinger, the brilliant Austrian physicist who ended his career in Dublin, posed a famous thought experiment. If a cat is trapped inside a box with a pill whose poison is released by the random firing of an atomic device, is the cat alive or dead before we open the box? His answer — that the cat exists in a probability state in which it is both alive and dead — is based on Werner Heisenberg's Uncertainty Principle and on the role of the observer in creating reality. (Schrödinger assumed that the cat was not an observer of its reality. This cat demurs.)

FIBONACCI SERIES: A series of numbers in which each is created by adding the two previous (1, 1, 2, 3, 5, 8, 11, and so forth) reveals the geometry of living things and can be used to map such diverse forms as a sunflower and a shell.

FIELD THEORY: It was thought for some centuries that a wave (including sound and light) had to propagate itself through a medium (air, water, and the now-discarded invisible "ether"). Fields are now known to be irreducible, simple physical entities, described by how they change and interact with other fields.

HIGGS' BOS'N: A hypothesized subatomic particle, this boson would be the heaviest ever known and would be responsible for creating matter. One of the Higgs' heavy mates, a boson called the quark, was named by physicist Murray Gell-Mann from a line in James Joyce's *Finnegans Wake*: "Three quarks for Mister Mark." In this poem, the Higgs' particle appears as a bos'n (boatswain), a sailing ship's officer.

THE POISED EDGE OF CHAOS: In the order/disorder continuum, the edge of chaos is also known as the area of complexity. Neither totally rigid nor totally unpredictable, it is the place where the greatest creative energy is found.